I0170479

Library of Congress Cataloging-In-Publication Data

Norman, Alexis

ISBN 978-0-9963595-2-8

A collection of letters organized by yours truly

If you think you are too

Small to make a difference,

You haven't spent the night

With a mosquito

-African Proverb

Table of Contents

Matter

Seeing you for the first time

Meeting you for the first time

A new love

A feeling that I've felt before but this time it's different

More serious

More content

A new love that speaks to me

The things you say touches me

The things you do entice me

Love me baby

Pieces

The glass drops, and glass is everywhere

This is just how I felt the day you left me

I slowly sweep up the glass, trying to get the pieces back together

Some of the pieces fit perfectly

While others don't

I miss being colorful

All around

Unknown

To swim down below

To fly to the top

To go where no man has gone before...

A tear drifts down my face

My dream takes me...surrounds me...soothes me

I'm floating in the middle of the sea

Swimming for love...floating for life

I'm one with this water

Taking on this never ending form

I AM STRONG

Finished with my diamonds

My form changes and I become a creature of the sky

The air dries me...but I'm still damp

So I fly to the tallest mountain...to relax

It seems that I'm equivalent to the sun

My hair is dry and I feel delightful...I take off

Arms at my side...I'm so graceful

But, my arms are tired so I fly to a well-known tree in my back garden

I hide so no one can see me...I climb down

Look at myself...and I'm satisfied with my days work

Tomorrow we'll see

You

Passion runs through my veins like flame when I think about you

I birthed you from my heart, I've created you in my mind

Manifested from just a thought

How amazing you are

Sun

Something

If I had to tell a tale I would speak of lost wonders

Wonders like the mermaid and the unicorn

So mysterious, so dreamy

So dreamy, it seems that these things can't be imagination

A figment of my imagination, no it's a worldwide imagination

Who says that the sailor is lost at sea

The only man left alive...all of his crew gone...Desert

He's floating along on an empty piece of metal

He's dreary from shock and right before he gives up a fish swims on his right side

Then his left, before long they're all around him...the sun is keeping him warm

The water sparkles like floating diamonds

A sharp wind comes, the waves

Nervous he shifts his body upward...too weak he fell back and off his wooden metal plate...into the water he goes

SPLASH

The sun has left and its pitch black

Dark moments past before he regains eye sight

The beautiful fish rubs his face, and has soothed him

These creatures are so friendly

He tries to speak but she silences him

She is as tall as the depth of the ocean...and as wide as the sea

Multicolor is she

They take him to a place down, down beneath

A kiss is passed and now he's able to breathe

Amazed by his sight, what could this be

Oh I must be dreaming he says because who would believe

He eats caviar and drinks the water of the sea

He hears singing in a distance

Singing like the birds sing to Jesus in the morning

Visit

He's at peace here, serenity

A thought crosses his mind and he begins to think about his family that he's left behind

Can I bring them down

No things like this mustn't be planned, it must just happen

The people notice a change and they to long for him to be happy

A sharp thunder below awakened the sea and he fell into a deep sleep

Depth and wide as the sea brought him to the shore

He awoke to a sound like no other, hot he begins to take off his shirt, rolled up his pants, and straight from heaven on a rainbow appeared a unicorn

The unicorn spoke to him and he obeyed

He rode for seven days and seven nights, his peers saw him approaching

They didn't see the unicorn, in their eyes he was walking

Their eyes were blinded by God, so they only saw what was necessary

When he awoke again for the third time his wife and daughter greeted him and as he looked upon their faces he told them

"You won't believe what I'm about to tell you", but before he started his story he asked the date and time

Twenty four hours had passed since he lost ship

This couldn't be

You know what, let me think about all that has happened and I'll tell you all about it later

Shameless

It's a shame what people will do for a little change

Shameless in will what has become of me, me as in my people

Not just "ethnic people"...but people in general...general population

The future population is this the best for my children...our children

Future is so unrealistic to me

The past is all I know or all that I'm sure of

So many things have happened, what type of things do we look for in the future

What will be good enough in the future if all things are accepted now

What will not be tolerated if all is now

Oh I'm so disgusted with society "at times like this" and "they say", "the children are the future"

What about the present

Desire

An agenda is my intention to seduce a young love

Is he...experienced

We'll see...when I see his face, I light up

Young crush...secret like...mutual...hesitant to find out

Eager to deliver...to please...to be pleased...to be wanted

Could this be...an agreed agenda that will work out for me

Identity

Without a face...without a trace of who I be

My past hidden by shame, disbelief

A black veil covers my face so no one can see me

Hiding in a mist

Black shadow, without a face

The fruit of me has grown

Grown into shame

Blameless I be, born in a shadow

A black veil covers me

Rocky

Thundering, Lighting...

A fire in the sea ignites from a hidden place

A rock...solid...strong...fierce...dark

That's my hidden space

Underneath my rock

Pushed

Asked to get a glimpse

Pull back fast cause it's still day light

I'm a night creature walking through the night

Waves relax and come to a halt

Still...until night

Secrets

The past...do we really want to no about the past

I feel that if we knew the real truth...we'd be even more confused then what we are today

If someone really told you...a whisper from a ghost of the past

Or even a secret passage in your back room

If it was available would you really take a step into the past

Would curiosity intrigue you that much or would you be scared

I mean we say we would want to no but actions speak louder than words

Focus...at night right before you dream

Think about what you're really asking

Lay back...relax and let your mind take you to an unknown destination

Now talk to me while you dream

Do you like what you see

Is it all you hoped it would be

Listen to your body, feel the time

Live there for a moment

Enjoy the good and the bad

Taste...smell...open your eyes...no don't shut them

See...water...live...attentive

Be grateful that this is only a dream for you because some have lived that reality

Torn

Many people asked how I felt that day

What if you received a call, a call that said your loved one wasn't there

What if one of your soul mates departed mentally, but not physically

What if you whispered in their ear "hold my hand", "squeeze my hand"

What if they were to squeeze your hand back

Well that's what happened to me

Its days like this that I miss you more than ever

Granny, it's so much joy in that name

"I remember EVERYTHING"

Stalked

I dream the dreams that only I can hear because I'm a silent voice

Standing out, just from what people see

Thinking they really know me

Being a silent voice can be a treasure if you can believe that

So much, I mean so many things kept inside

Debating with yourself, talking to self

Being all by myself

You...I say none of these things, I remain silent

I'm silent

I know love

If I could have both I would

Two different types of love from both, multiples

My chocolate delight, my vanilla sunshine

Yet I'm still too silent to speak the truth about both

History

Suppose I gather everybody here to tell a story. Let's say I asked you "what's your story"

What would you say

Would you tell me your story or someone else's, being truthful

If my story relates to your life would you use it as an example to cover yours up or would you be honest

I'll tell you my story once you tell me yours

A story has a beginning and an end

How can a story be complete with us still here

Who will write the end to my story, your story if we're sitting right here

Story this story that everything can be a story and now that I'm gone I ask you again to tell me your story

Tell me from the beginning to the end so I'll understand our story

Folk Lore

There's a true story about something that never happened

Like many days it won't stop raining, looking out the window I say "I might as well get dressed up"

So I did

I get dressed up in my life, because yesterday I rejected me

Looking out the window, it's so sunny, but a second ago it was raining

My life can be so much at times, times like this

Right now today, maybe tomorrow things will change

Today I awoke to thunderstorms and clouds, once again I got dressed up in my favorite suit

To go nowhere but here

Rain, rain, it can really ruin your day

I watch the news and the weather man says that today's high will be 80 degrees

Sunny, warm and clear, but why is it so much rain and cloudiness in my life

There's a sweet smell coming from my basement

I follow that scent to see what it is

FIRE! FIRE!

It's so hot but I just can't move

Frozen in time right where I stand

Void, anger, hurt, deception is hardly what I feel

Words written on paper can't express what I feel

Black, blackness is all I see

I look to my left, my right and I shrink to my feet

The ashes blow both ways

I look and I still can't see my face

Void, hurt, sad

Sleep

Ricky Valquez is waiting impatiently to visit Mari'

On July 14, 2003 there was a strange accident that was Ricky's fault

Patiently standing in the waiting room Ricky has all the time in the world to think about what has happened

But the only thing he can remember is the bright lights

It seems they were everywhere, coming from every angle

Why am I not hurt

Nurse Ann comes out to let Ricky know that he can now see the patient

As Ricky enters the rooms he begins to feel something, what is it that he's feeling

Sitting the flowers down Ricky looks over at Mari', what have I done

He grabs her hand and begins to talk about today and how beautiful it is outside

Considering that Mari' hasn't seen the sunlight for three months, since the accident

Three months in a coma seems like an eternity I wonder who that is that's speaking to me

If I could open my eyes I would maybe recognize the face

Oh! Who am I kidding, where I'm at now is very comfortable

His touch is very nice but it seems so familiar

This is strange, too strange

I wish he'd just shut up and let me rest

Look at me now, I had the perfect life

CEO of my company, no children, just me, my money and friends

All I can remember is lights, lights everywhere, coming from different angles

Waking up out the coma nurse Ann comes in to let me know I will survive

I look to the woman of my dreams who has been by my side since the beginning

I see life from her side and I can now say that I truly understand

Awake

Now I am truly awake

Wonders

I don't want to say my faith is leaving me, but God you know goodness and perfectness

Two beings so small, so fragile, so perfect

Beautiful to my eyesight is she

She's so beautiful to me, and he's so handsome to her

Perfect like I don't see, like I'll never see

Dampness on this sheet from my sadness, my confusion, my anger, my frustration, my anticipation, my determination, my will

Please give me the answers I want to hear

Please give me one hundred percent of negativity, "you know what I mean"

Silence, I speak silence, mute

I move mutely, "is that even a word,"

I move mutely around and I smile constantly so no one will see my sad eyes

If people only knew a day and the struggle of a "privileged girl" like myself

It's so very much overrated, what I wouldn't do for true happiness for them

For true love for me, I mean I put on a great tough girl façade but I want what every girl wants

Love from a handsome prince

To give myself to him like I've gave myself to no other

For him to give himself to me like no other

Let's love, and make love…until….until I tire

Not tired of you but tired from you

A constant pleasure is what I want him to be

Not just pleasure but I want him to enjoy me

Strong willed

I'm not your average girl, I'm above

Fly

Once a beehive

Standing alone

Growing and growing

With more and more honey bees

One bee

This bee

Striving

Sucking all the honey out of this beehive

The beehive falls

The bees all scatter

What happened to the honey bee

I'm Up

Wake up…wake up

This sound coming from beneath me

I sit up in my bed and look to my left "your right"

Immediately I begin to get dressed because my friend has come over

After I'm one hundred percent ready it's time to go, right

Wrong

I'm still in the bed, why is this

I know I can move because I sat up

Wake up…wake up

I am up I shout, but no one can hear me

I'm looking in the mirror brushing my hair

Leave me alone I say, but I'm interrupted by a strange noise that's coming from downstairs

This has to be impossible because my parents are at work, basically I'm home alone "I guess"

I stand at the top of the stairs, who's their I say just above a whisper

But no one answers me

You could say excuse you, I think to myself, "She sure is rude"

As I go downstairs, it seems to be a party in my house, damn

I'm really upset now, I begin screaming "get out of my house right now"

 But everyone seems to be in their own world

I walk up to a man and he's looking right at me but he says nothing

These people are so rude, I'm only a kid

I'm tired of people treating me like this, some baby

I'm thirteen years old, I'm basically an adult

Right

Why are they all dressed alike

Maybe I've been asleep for too long because black seems to be the color

I'd better go upstairs and change before someone notices that I'm still in my p.j.'s

I'm back upstairs in my room looking in my closet, that's funny my closet is empty

Wake up, wake up, I hear my mother say

But she couldn't be talking to me because I'm already up

I suddenly feel funny, maybe tired, I really don't know

Light, that's what I see and that's how I feel "light," like I'm floating

I keep saying I'm up, not realizing that I'm up here alone

Yet I don't feel alone, theirs someone with me in this house

Here, Now

Once you were here, things were nice

Now that you're gone I've changed my life

To once one knows, only others don't

One's trust shared with that special someone

Once you're here now you're not

Trust is taken away by death

When death is conquered everyone has a question

They're all left unanswered

The wise man said "no young blood trust your heart shall be the key to you"

Maybe not yours but there's victory

Your life is conquered by what you see

Remember others might not be so strong

Everyone needs someone to lean gone. You're gone

Love

For a time we had a friendship

Love

We shared something so magical, for the thought of us departing is like destruction

A magic trick gone wrong

I often think of our time shared

The intimacy, not so much physically but mentally

You knew me and I knew you

Who have these two people become

What has become of me

Enemies

No

Friends

No

It's as if nothing ever occurred between you and me

What could this be

Wish

Coming to your room baby

You know how much I've been missing you, early in the day

Contemplating calling you

Wondering if you miss me as much as I miss you, baby

What are we going to do

Imagination begins to flow

Images appear right before my eyes

I begin to interact with those images

Feeling a strange, void

Awakening from a deep sleep, and you're not even here with me, in my room

Confused I am because I could have sworn I heard your voice calling me babe

What a day

Me

Who can see the sadness in my eyes

No one

These tears that I cry, just like things around me

I don't know what's going on with me, I'm so confused

What should I do

I can't write because I keep crying

What am I crying for

Why am I sad

What brings me joy

My mother's happiness makes me so

A Thought of Thoughts

Look down and shine on me

Can't you see my sad eyes

If I had one last thing to say to you

What would it be

I can't remember the last two months before you left

After you left

Shine some sunlight

On my sad eyes

Mad

Anger is what I feel for this anonymous person

There is a woman. A boy, a man and a girl

The life of this young girl seems to be good on the outside

But on the inside her heart is hurt

Hurt from this man's love

It isn't there and she is confused

So much hate

Love from the woman that is there

The girl knows the love from this woman has to be enough

But sometimes she feels different

And this boy, this pissy ass boy, is not helping the situation at all

What's the girl to do

This life is some bullshit

Such words from a young lady

Who cares

Who can judge me

Not you

Not me

No one

Anger is a process of elimination of who will go first

So who can waste time with others

You yourself have to leave

Whatever

In heart or flesh

You and only you know your anger

Just know your limits

Alone

In my house alone

I hear a knock at the door

Who is it

No one's their

Could I be going crazy missing you

I hear a noise in the other room

When I came in

No one was their

I'm going crazy insane

At the end of the night after I had a stank ass attitude I was left alone

Dear Angel

How are you

I'm doing just fine

Missing and missing you being mine

There's a cloud that's come down and sweeps me away

This place is so light

Seeing nothing

Feeling everything

Open your hand

Set me free

Who knew that you were holding me all this time

Hidden

Thundering, lighting...a fire in the sea ignites from a hidden place

A rock...solid...strong...fierce...dark

That's my hiding space...underneath my rock

Pushed, asked to get a glimpse

Pull back fast...cover it

Still daylight

I'm a night creature

A creature walking through the night

Be patient

A change is about to come

Nothing can stop this change

"Good Change"

Voice

I try to say things out loud

Hoping that you hear

Wishing my voice could travel to you through the wind

Wishing I could fly over your house like a bird

Around

I'm on an emotional roller coaster

 I Feel that no one can/will ever understand me

I feel so alone in this world of mine

The worst thing in your life is to love someone who doesn't love you back

Or love you in your special way

I love this boy

See'er

I'm your secret watcher

Where you go...I go

Wherever you be...I be

Secretly waiting and longing to see you

I lie high in my nest...even a bird like me needs rest

I chirp at your window pane

Do you know it's me babe

Every night when you lye asleep, I watch you from your window pane

This is what excites me

The fact that you don't know that I see you everyday

I'm always watching you babe

I'm your secret watcher

Now watch me fly away

Shh

Be silent and listen

Listen to what you know is true

Listen to what you know is real

Not the things that appear real

But true honesty

So many things have caught our attention

But focus

Focus on self and not self's belongings

To materialistic

Am I all that is said about me, because I know me one hundred percent

My own will, will...again

Bittersweet trust

For You

I wish you knew the sacrifices I make for you

Everything I'm willing to give up because I'm so much in love with you

I now know what true love is because I lost love

I've gained knowledge on what loving someone really is

And I do love you

I do love you

Everything that is in you is love to me

Everything that's in you is love for me

1st

Theirs a first for everything

A first thought

A first love

A first kiss

Why not make your first one to remember

And chose a first that will last always

Dark

Silent water...Dark Ocean

Mysterious just like the sky

Creature of land is me, but oh do I long to travel the sea

Travel just like the planes travel the sky

Do I dare dream a though like this

Questions

So many questions do I have

Questions that will change my life and answers that will cure my soul

Make a Claim

To claim what's yours you must take a stand

Have a voice

Don't just speak...be heard

Loud and clear

Be truthful to yourself...at all times

Never lose what drove you to do such magnificent things

Remain neutral and cool

Respect at all times...but be observant

Be patient

When you work for your blessings...you'll appreciate them until the end

About Today

I can give you something to think about

It all depends on what you're in the mood for

What will it be today

Because if it's anything like last night then I'm more than willing

I'm able and ready

I'll be the subject for any test

Anything that you want to explore

Your deepest thoughts and fantasies will come true

I'm willing...ready and wanting

Wanting you just as much as you're wanting me

K.I.S.S

All At Once

At a time where peace meets hostility

Theirs conflict

So much conflict...confusion...turmoil

Silent

Speak later...listen now

At a time where peace meets hostility

Confusion...which one to chose

Which one is strong

It depends

This very thought is conflicting, feeling both

This is where peace meets hostility

See

If you looked into my eyes

What would you see

A blank page

Waiting for you to write all your desires about me

It's your own canvas

Self-creation

I'm allowing myself to be everything you write down

I'll try to be

Entament

Kissing

Threw against the wall

Passionate pain

Touching

Rubbing

Searching for ecstasy

Learning each other's bodies

Your hand...my body...becomes one

Never thought that I could feel this much pleasure at one time

The way you handled me in a ruff...tender way

So amazing

Heaven

Whisper

If you could look into my eyes

When solo becomes duet

My heart of ice is melted

And you are my son

You sent me your warm rays

My cold heart is gone

My days of rain has ended

Yes you shined your light

You came when I needed you

Baby, you are alright

It Happened

I found it hard to stay away

And every night I prayed

That you'd come back to me

We had a solid love

I thought couldn't end

And before we were lovers we were very good friends

I thought because of this our love would never end

But it ended quickly as it began

I found it hard to stay away

And every night I prayed that you'd come back to me

What we had was strong

I thought it would last...so long

Until you said, good bye

In fact I even cried

Refreshed

The wind knows my name

Why do you call

Have I did something wrong

I don't think so at all

Who else do you call...do you call others

You call everyone

No one calls you

First you blow slowly

Then you move smooth

It all depends on your moving mood

But when you blow wind wild you move in the storm

Why do you call me

Have I did something wrong

Keep on calling me

I won't answer the call

I will pretend you're not calling at all

Yes I can hear you

Call

After me calling you

After I'm writing you...a love letter

Booh

Why you want to call me now

Why you want to change things now

Why did you put me through all this pain

Why now...why now

I remember your sexy ways

The special way you looked at me...

Times

After all these years you're not in my life

I've dreamed of this moment for a very long time

Now that you're here words can't come to mind

So much time

Where did you go

Why did you leave

Just don't go, don't tell me no

Don't walk out that door, don't leave me alone

After all these years you're staying home

Time to think

What to say

You're standing here

We're face to face now

Let me think, I know what to say

I love you

In each and every way possible

Whatever it is, you're not going anywhere tonight

Really

How can I miss what I never had

How could you make me then forsake me

How could you not give yourself to me

All my life I've waited until the tears left

Then I began to see clearly

All those years you just hurt me

Why was I not pretty enough for you

Was I a mistake for you

Or was I just not you

You were so selfish in all the things you did

Va'se

A beautiful va'se

Painted with rainbow colors

From a distance you see only the beautiful colors

When you look closer you can see the inside is just one color

The color of pain

What color is pain if you see nothing there

A beautiful va'se

Alone there

Surrounded

When I sit on top of the water

Light in body

Strong in spirit

A will in my heart

In the middle of the sea

It's just you and me God

I love you and being here is your word

TRUE

Us

Our first kiss

Our first touch

Nervousness was all over me

You touch

I react

The way you feel against me

Kissing my neck

Remembering when you first got me...
when I first felt the pleasure of you against me

Oh, what a feeling

Speak

Love is a word

Spoken but not unchosen

But decisions you make throughout life

What is life

Your definition of love

Love is soft, cuddly

Love is your voice, oh boy so sweet

Love is you and me being one

A thought

A wonder

How can I love you so much

Everything in me is loving love

I love your walk...your smile

The way you look when you're full of life

Some of my best moments were spent with you

Unforgettable things you gave me

And boy o boy I'm glad I spent those moments with you instead of someone else

My only regret at this point is that...

Silent

A love unchosen

Words unspoken

Everything all given

Everyone knows

Where love falls

Who's to say were the ending is

Ended one day

Everything

Found hanging in a room

Love died for you

And in the pocket of love the note was found and it read

"I was sent here to you, I died for you, I loved you, and damn I can't believe I'm dead because of you"

p.s. suicide

Shadow

In a mirror there's an image

But who do I see

This strange woman looking back at me

Seeing my future...my past

Wondering how I got there

After so many things

There's something special about who I see

This woman is amazing looking back at me

I need her strength

I need her courage

It's my future

My past

Willingly

Serious

If someone can make you angry they can control you

My 1st Love

When I was sick you nurtured me

When I needed an ear you listened to me

When I needed discipline you gave it to me

In more ways than physical

Once again I need you

Ok for now

But who knows about tomorrow

The best is yet to come

Needing you my first love

Question

I've got a question...do you mind if I ask

Would this last

How long do I have to be with you

I think you know how I feel

You know my love is real

Let's take time to talk about our future

Do you want to know what I'm going to ask

If you do then let's settle it

I'd like to know

Do you think I'm a girl you like

Do you think we'll always last

Do you think we can have a future

Do you think about it babe

Do you think about all these things

But most of all do you think about me babe

I noticed that you look as if you have something to say

Then...you know what to do

Answer

Girl you know I love you, and anything you ask I'll do

But I've got a couple of questions for you

Do you love me babe

Cause if you do then marry me

I can picture my life just like this

This is my wish

Do you think we can be true to one another

Do you think

Do you think we can be true to one another

Do you think you can get along with my mother

Do you think this will always be...because I never thought you'd chose me

Tell me babe

But most of all do you think about me babe

I think I've found my true love...you are everything I've dreamed of

I think we can be together always

Now look at us babe

P.M.S

Like the stars in the sky

Love Love

Like the sun to the moon

Love Love

Like the ocean to the waves

Love Love

As hard as it is to say goodbye

One last night with you would be alright

You've brought so much joy to my life

I've often wondered why

Do you know...how I feel...your love

Give it to me once again and I'll be more than ready to receive it

My heart is racing...pounding like a thunderstorm

Waterfalls from my eyes

Blinded

To teary to see what's in front of me

Love Love

Sneaky

A witch

A spell

A curse of love

A man

A world

Full of hate

Entwined together

Could this be

What has happened

This young man has put a spell on me

Famous

Glamourous

Sure we live the glamourous life

But when it comes to being you

Always respect yourself

I Use To Care

I don't care about him

Yes, I care about you

You are the one I want to give my love to

He didn't care about me

Not like I care about you

Can I have all your love

And yes I'm ready to share to

I don't care about him, he played to many games

I care about you

With you things changed

He didn't care about me, like you do

You are the one I gave all my love to

I don't care about him

He played me out

Only lies came from his mouth

I don't care about him

I Cried

To once again I cried

I cried for love

I cried for frustration

Anticipation

I cried for love

I spoke to my mother, she's always an excellent ray of sun, even on a cloudy day like this

I cry like the sky on a raining day

I cry for the past, present and future

Who cries for me if I don't cry at all

Who cares for me, really

Who really understands me and the emotions I feel

If I told

If I tell what would I say

Well is all, I cry just as I cried before

P.I.N.K

Pretty is naturally Kool

P.I.N.K describes this

When you see this color it means so much

Self-explanatory per say

It's more the a color, it's a movement that speaks to all who see and wear P.I.N.K

What color signifies you

What color makes you look good

Make sure you represent an on-going change in life

A Time

Baby when I think about everything between us

It's more than a dream

It's more than a crush

Sometimes I think I'm crazy, being in love with you

Writing you a letter is not the same

I can tell you I love you in many ways

Loving everything about you babe

Making love comes naturally

Babe it's you

Eagle

A sorcerer of the sky...

King of its kind...

So high...

Fly...

Above...

And...

Beyond...

Thoughts...Wonders...

Images....Senses...

He's alert...Attacks...

Catches his prey...Beautiful he is...

Adjacent to the sun...

Moves with the clouds in motion...

Largest of its kind...

Eagle...

Handle It

So many emotions

Emotions that I feel I can't handle

I feel so many things

But which of these things will consume me

Hate

Love

Romance

Un-forgiveness

Which one do I chose

I hate the fact that I left you

I love the time we shared

A romance no man could understand un-forgiveness for you leaving me

For a short time I hated you

I know that was unfair judgment but that was the only way for me to deal with your leaving me

My question to you is

Would you have stayed if you could

Now I'm wondering why I feel all these emotions

Around

The beginning

The middle

The end

Starts over again

Circle

Ride

I'm thinking of a place for us to go

How about a bus ride to the library

Or how about going out for a bite to eat

Just you and me

The arcade would be a special treat all for you booh

That would be the best day from me to you

I'm never forget our first bus ride

A special time for us to be together

The smile on your face is something I will never forget

Beautiful "Interlude"

Beautiful person

Beautiful place

In my heart and everywhere in space

All by Myself

Alone, thinking about my time spent with you

Alone imagining you

Dreaming you

Creating you in my ultimate fantasy

Concentrating

Putting all of my thoughts into you

Into this

Into us

Creating an untouched atmosphere where only you and I can survive

Alone...thinking...wishing

Dreaming all night about you

Story-Tale

For you to sit and tell me a story is asking me my story

Your confidence is my confidence

You telling me is me telling myself

Especially if I'm writing this on paper

I guess if I re-read all that I ever wrote I would know a lot about me

I don't know His Name

The first time I saw him I didn't know we would fall in love

I talked to him for a little while

He left with a happy smile

The second time I saw him he spilled all his problems to me

But what could I do

How could I solve them

I asked him to slow down and to please start over again

That's when he told me she needed a special friend

The third time that I saw him I knew what he was thinking of

A blind man could see that he wanted my love

I let him ask the question, I knew he had it planned

He came straight out and asked me to be his loving woman

I haven't seen him sense

With him I played his game

He told me all about him

But he forgot to mention his name

For Me

This is what he has to do to me

He has to rub and hold my body

Treat me tender

Make me feel warm

Be my shelter from the storm

Stop the rain ...take me in

Love every moment...from beginning to end

Trust and love me for me

This is what he has to do for me

This is what he has to do for me

He has to kiss my body

Hold me close and kiss me down

Go round and round

Take me from all life's pain

Love me down...but never the same

Give his love to only me

This is what he has to do for me

I Know

Baby I know what makes you hot

I know where to kiss

I know how to rub the spots that others have missed

Kisses all over your body

Just drives you wild

Foreplay in such a way that makes you quiver on the inside

The rhythm, method nice and slow

Makes your body vibrate frontward and sideways

Ease your body aches

Whatever fashion you prefer

You let me know the style

That makes your inner body quiver

Private places where only I kiss

Makes goose bumps arrive on your body...where I kiss

Helps you feel alive

I know all the corners to cut

I know when and where, to make you let go-I know

Stormy Winds

The wind is calling out your name

But I can't see your face

When I look into the clouds I can see a trace

A trace of your face

Cause the clouds are trying to form

The same thing that killed our relationship

And baby this is a storm

What made the storm come, was it the weather

I thought that we would stay together forever

Like a sea ship caught in a tide

Turning into a circle where could we hide

As our ship sank, I knew you could swim

When your head came above water, you were with her

The wind is calling your name

But I can't see, you going with her and leaving me

Caught on a raft, nowhere to turn

I quickly began to swim

Funny sometimes how you learn

Stuck in the middle, I almost gave up

A tied carried me to land

Yes, I was in luck

Caught in a storm

Some may know what I'm talking about

I'm caught in a storm of love

Constantly

I found it hard to stay away

And every night I prayed

That you'd come back to me

We had a solid love

I thought, could never end

And before we were lovers we were friends

I thought because of this that our love would never end

But it ended just as quickly as it began

I found it hard to stay away

And every night I prayed that you'd come back to me

What we had was strong

I thought it would last long

Until you said goodbye

In fact I even cried

Soul

Dark soul, Dark soul

Who calls my name

Creatures of the sea speak to me

My dreams haunt me

A past so mystique attached to my soul

But not my body

A stranger I am to me

A summer day bores and frustrates me

A winter day soothes me

The cold that is in me is oh so relaxing

Back home to my roots

Yea, that sounds good to me

I

Yea and swim

Prayer

Jesus

Sweet Jesus can I have a word with you

So much

So much is going on and I don't know what to do

You told me

You told me I could always call on you

So Jesus

So Jesus tell me what it is you want me to do

So many times I was lost and I didn't know what to do

Two paths which do I chose

You told me to follow in your footsteps and everything would be cool

The path I chose was due to understanding

So Jesus you've blessed me so much

My mind and my body is all you

Every bit of hurt you've been through for me

Sweet Jesus you are wonderful

But if I could be perfect I would

Jesus you confront me through the cloudy storms

And it was through the storms that I saw the sun

This world is such a terrible place

I'm glad I have you to guide me

For business inquires contact xitlane@gmail.com